HAUNTS
OF
THE CASHTOWN INN

Compiled
by
Suzanne Gruber
Bob Wasel

Published
by
Bob Wasel

COVER DESIGN BY:
Bryce Carpenter
Bob Wasel

SKETCHES BY:
Tom Winter, Jr.
Time Line Designs

Printed in the United States of America

DEDICATION

To Mom and Dad, Jeanne and Ali, Judy, Roxana, Ellen and Bobby, Natalie and John...and, especially, Bob.
SG

To Renée, Rhonda, and Robert
BW

ACKNOWLEDGMENTS

Special thanks to Scott Alderman, Judith Banasiak, Bryan Barr, Howard Calp, T. Chillemi, Teresa Chillemi, Daniel Crowley, Erin Crowley, Linda DeCecchis, Steven DeCecchis, Shelley B. DeGripp, Mary Jo Egbert, Ralph Franzenc, John Kamerer, Andrew Keyser, Roger Koehler, Jeff Lloyd, Lisa Lloyd, Carla R. Meinecke, Eric W. Meinecke, Erika Millen, Greg Millen, Allan Moore, Donnel Moore, Charles G. Morrongiello, Michelle R. Morrongiello, Michael A. Mowrey, Ashley Ott, Rhonda Ott, Stephanie Ott, P.R., Carol Pindell, John B. Puet, Michelle Puet, Brian D. Seibel, Wilda D. Seneriz, Jeff Shey, Bonnie Stackhouse, and Robert E. Tanice. And especially to Dennis, Eileen, and Jason Hoover for all their help.

© Carol Shaffer 1996

Historic Cashtown Inn 1797

1325 Old Rt. 30
P.O. Box 103
Cashtown, PA 17310
(717) 334-9722

High St.

← W Rt. 30 Gettysburg →

Old Rt. 30

INTRODUCTION

Soon after becoming the most recent "caretakers" of the Cashtown Inn during the spring of 1996, we decided to place Guest Log books in each of our seven rooms. It has been fascinating to read the supernatural experiences that take place in each room, so when Bob Wasel suggested turning the entries into a book, we agreed, hoping others would enjoy them as much as we have.

Long before the Cashtown Inn became famous for its ghosts, it was well-known as a source of hospitality. Built around 1797 as the first stagecoach stop west of Gettysburg on the Gettysburg-Chambersburg turnpike, the inn immediately became a place for lodging, food, and drink. The Conestoga wagon masters driving the turnpike would shout to each other, "Remember up ahead that cash town," because innkeeper Peter Marks accepted only cash as payment for services. Hence, the name Cashtown was in place by 1821.

In October of 1862, J.E.B. Stuart's Confederate troops raided the inn, and the following June of 1863, General A.P. Hill made the inn his headquarters prior to the Battle of Gettysburg. The famous Confederate soldier who is still seen in our hallways and in Room #4 is probably the young man who was mortally wounded up the pike by one of the hotel customers during the last week of June.

In the 20th century, the inn was used as a restaurant and dance hall, and since 1987, as a county inn offering food, spirits, and lodging.

We hope you enjoy the stories in this book, keeping in mind that we have much more to fear from the living than from the dead.

Cashtown innkeepers,
Dennis and Eileen Hoover

ROOM 2
BRIG. GEN. JOHN IMBODEN

November 8-10, 1996: We have had a marvelous getaway weekend here. The charm and ambiance of this historic inn, combined with the gastronomic delights from your kitchen, were exceeded only by the warm hospitality extended by the Hoovers. Our rest was disturbed only once by a "visitor." Thank you—we shall return!

November 12, 1996: As I was sleeping, something awakened me. I felt something heavy laying on my back as I was curled somewhat sideways with my husband. It felt as if *someone* was on top of both of us. Several moments later, it felt as if "he" went through my body! It is difficult to describe the feeling; it seemed like applesauce going through a strainer. At one point, for the briefest moment, I felt terrible pain—as if I felt pain from some deep wound on "his" body. And then, I felt "him" leave my body, out towards the door. As soon as "he" left, I immediately asked my husband if he had felt that! He said, "no." I laid quietly for another several minutes before describing to him what had just happened.

I was not frightened, although never before did I have an experience like that! It was exactly 2:36 a.m.

Later in the night, I awoke to a distant snoring. I don't know if it was "him" or someone in the next room.

Our second night was uneventful. I will never forget my stay here at the Cashtown Inn.

> *The first week we lived in the Cashtown Inn, I looked over my shoulder everywhere I went. Eventually realizing that I would have to make peace with the spirits of the inn, I verbally approached them with the following request: "I don't care how many of you are here. But can we make a deal? I won't bother you if you don't bother me."*
> *So far it has worked.*
>
> —Eileen Hoover

November 24, 1996: We came as a group of four to seek spirits. I brought Mardi Gras beads as a novelty to attract the spirits. I laid the beads on the dresser as we unpacked our bags. We were in and out of the room several times during the course of the first day. On two distinct occasions, "someone" moved the gold beads from the dresser to the plate with the heart. Seeking more thrills...at about 3 a.m., I removed the gold beads from the dresser and placed them on the floor behind a tree. At about 7 a.m., I found them around the doll in the cradle. Here is where they will stay—my gift to the spirits!

Had a great stay here and, of course, will definitely return!

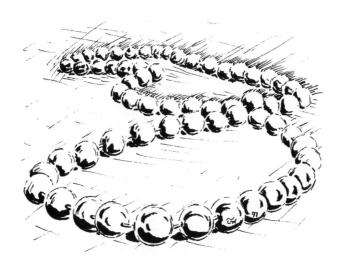

December 28, 1996: Awoke at 2:35 a.m. feeling rest-less—unable to sleep. I had a heavy feeling on my chest and stomach, which I attributed to the wonderful food and drink. I listened for horses or moaning [or other strange sounds]. Did not hear any, although I *did* hear a soft snoring sound that continued until I fell asleep. (Possibly a guest in the next room sleeping soundly?)

In the morning, my husband told me of a similar account written in the journal in November 1996, and I be-gan to wonder if we, too, had been "visited." At breakfast, Eileen told me that there was no guest in the next room. Could it be??!!

Wonderful stay! Great food and marvelous hospitality. Will return!

*F**ebruary 8, 1997:*** We have returned for our fourth visit to the Cashtown Inn. We are staying in Room 2 this time, but we have previously stayed in Rooms 1, 3, and 6. When we were in Room 3 back in October, nothing really happened except a weird dream. Since I had a strange dream again last night, I decided to log them both.

In Room 3, I had a dream that my husband got up in the middle of the night to use the bathroom. When he shut the bathroom door, I felt cold and scared. Something dragged me out of bed and onto the floor—sheets, blankets, and all. I fought, but ended up on the floor anyway. I tried to call out to my husband for help, but nothing came out! Suddenly, a totally black figure appeared. It stood above me.

I could make out that it was a man wearing a three-quarter length coat and a tall hat. He leaped over me (remember, I was on the floor) onto the bed, then was gone.

My dream here in Room 2 was a short one, too. My husband and I were lounging around when lights began to go on and off. We looked at each other and laughed nervously. Then "something" not visible jumped onto the bed with us! We saw the impression of the "something" on the bed. Then "it" seemed to enter my husband. He went limp and turned really red in the face. I took him in my arms and tried to snap him out of it. His eyes just rolled around in his head. I got so scared, I woke up!

We both heard bumps in the night in the hallway—long, unnatural footsteps that faded away. Then twice, I heard something that sounded like someone had bumped into a chair or table, but no footsteps—just a bump. Oh, well, someday I'll get the scare I've been waiting for!

ℱebruary 28-March 2, 1997: The radio shut off by itself twice! Heard what seemed to be laughing coming from the upper right hand corner of the room. It lasted about ten seconds, then faded. Other than that, everything was pretty normal. I slept great; however, my wife was afraid to shut her eyes!

> *While doing late-night book work, Chef George Keeney and his wife heard the sound of crashing china in the kitchen. Certain that all the plates had fallen to the floor, they rushed into the kitchen...only to find nothing out of place!*

ℳarch 14, 1997 {Day 1}: ("To the Spirits...we welcome all of you with blessings and open minds and hearts...") My husband and I are here for our second visit. On our first visit (November 1996), we stayed in Room 5. A lot of strange things happened during our stay back then...the porch swing violently swinging with no wind;

15

running in the halls; flickering lights in the hallway; sounds of laughter of young girls, running, playing. I wanted to try a new room this time.

We were here the weekend the Mardi Gras beads kept moving (the patrons of this room at the time showed us). Well, I will keep a log each night for strange, paranormal sightings or sounds. Stay tuned...(*Note: My cousin and his wife are staying in Room 1. They just told me that "someone" keeps moving his ditty bag from the chair to the far side of the bed on the floor!*)

*M*arch 15, 1997 {Day 2-a.m.}: Just came up from the parlor downstairs. Went in the bathroom to brush my teeth and a foul odor of perspiration and smelly feet permeated the room! I called my husband in to smell the odor, but just as he came in the door, the odor disappeared!

*M*arch 15, 1997 *{Day 2-p.m.}:* Today, we went to a psychic for a reading. Excellent day! At night, we went through the battlefield. When we got back, we felt very uneasy. Something kept waking me up! Not a very good sleep. I kept telling "them" to leave me alone, but it felt like someone was watching me! We had some scary moments during our stay, but we *will* return!!

ROOM 3
LT. GEN. AMBROSE P. HILL

May 15-17, 1996: A strange noise awakened my wife and me from a dead sleep our first night at the inn. The noise sounded to me like a light tapping. It started, stopped, and started again. My wife thought it was the sound of someone rocking in a chair…a sound not unlike a mother trying to put her newborn back to sleep in the middle of the night. Nevertheless, the sound kept us up most of the night. So which explanation is correct?

May 29, 1996 {Day 1}: At 8:50 p.m., we returned to this room to retire for the evening. Upon locking the door, I noticed that the door to the bathroom started to open by itself...it opened approximately a foot. We set up our video recorder and I have my camera ready, as we are expecting a very interesting night!

May 30, 1996 {Day 2}: As we begin our departure preparations this morning, we have nothing to report in the way of anything unusual while we slept last night. The normal sounds of an old house settling down after everyone retires for the night was all that we heard, with the exception of something I heard just before I dozed off. I heard footsteps in the hall coming up to the door of our room and then retreating from it. There were no other guests lodging here last night, so we cannot attribute the sounds to human footsteps. We saw nothing but the aforementioned bathroom door. As we depart this morning, we will be photographing the areas of this lovely old establishment and maybe we will have a picture or two to send back here with some "ghosts" on them!

A late-night menu-planning session between the innkeeper and the chef was interrupted by the sound of footsteps descending the stairs from the second floor. The innkeeper called out to her husband, thinking it was him because no guests were staying at the inn that night. There was no response, even after a second call, and the footsteps continued. The innkeeper walked into the parlor to investigate, but no one was on the stairs (and hubby was in bed asleep)!

June 21, 1996 {Day 1}: We are celebrating our tenth wedding anniversary. We eagerly entered our room and relaxed for a while, since we don't get to do much of that with work and four kids! We left around 3 p.m. with no ghostly experiences. It is now about 11 p.m. and we are just spending some more relaxing time together. Soon we will go to sleep...

We did not know, however, that Room 3 is the most famous room for ghostly encounters.

June 22, 1996 {Day 2}: During the night, my wife and I heard noises that might have been of a ghostly nature. I heard something hit the floor near the rocker. My wife said she heard a faint squeak coming from somewhere outside the room. Before going to sleep, I heard a very faint noise that sounded like fiddles. When I raised my head from the pillow, I no longer heard it. I kept hearing it until I finally went to sleep. During the night, I definitely heard children laughing and talking outside the door. There was only one other guest at the inn...an older man who was staying here alone.

One more thing to note: My wife had a half-filled glass of water on the nightstand when we went to sleep. This morning, it was empty. (She does not remember drinking it!!)

June 23, 1996 {Day 3}: Well, our stay here at the Cashtown Inn is coming to a close. No strange things to report...except that last night I awoke to notice that the air conditioner was off. I woke up my wife to ask what had happened to it. She was about to answer when, in two seconds, it came back on. When it did come back on, I got goose flesh! I know it is a common occurrence for air conditioners to do that, but it was just so strange that it came on right when I asked about it!

July 1, 1996: My husband, who never remembers his dreams, remembered a dream he had last night. There was a tap on the door. He got out of bed to see who was there, and when he opened the door, there were three men standing in the doorway. Then, in a flash, they were gone! After 32 years of marriage, this is the only dream he has ever recalled. I can only ask...*Was it a dream???*

July 2, 1996 {Day 1}: My husband and I arrived late in the afternoon today. After getting settled in, he decided to leave the room. As he closed the door to the room, the bathroom door opened fully. I do not recall if the door was fully shut at the time. Was this caused by the wind from the room door closing, or a wandering spirit happy that my husband left the room?

July 3, 1996 {Day 2}: The strangest occurrence happened last evening after we went to sleep. My husband awoke in the middle of the night to discover the air conditioner was off. This happened to us earlier in the day on the "save" economy setting, so we put it in the "on" position that night. He continued to wake up every hour until the next morning. He informed me that I was tossing and turning all night. At one point, he said he tried to stop me from moving about, and he put his hand on mine, discovering that my hands were crossed in front of me. Upon realizing this, he said it felt as though the hand slipped away, that it felt clammy and cold, and that it was not mine. It kept him up all night.

I believe the spirit of this room is much more comfortable with women, so men beware!

July 22, 1996: I was awakened at 2 a.m. by a noise in the far corner of the room. When I looked up, the rocking chair was moving to and fro. Later in the morning, my wife and I were both awakened by a loud noise coming from the same area. The chair, however, was not rocking this time.

Twice yesterday I heard a woman's voice utter something I could not make out. The first time, I was just opening the door from the hall. I heard a sharp voice off to my left...but no one was there.

Later, as I was getting ready for bed, I heard the voice again, coming from the area by the front windows. My wife was in the bathroom, so I know it wasn't her!

July 28, 1996: Spent the day at Gettysburg and arrived at the inn at 6:30 p.m. When we went to bed last night and turned out all the lights, my wife said that for several minutes, the little light that existed in the room seemed to dim even more, then return to normal, then within seconds, it dimmed again. This continued for several minutes.

I did not experience this myself and my wife seemed upset that only she could notice it. Strange!

July 30, 1996 {Day 1}: We arrived at the inn for a long-anticipated vacation. I, enjoying history as I do, read as much as I could find about the Cashtown Inn. Unfortunately, a little wisdom can be a dangerous thing.

As we went to bed, every story I'd read kept going through my mind and I kept thinking, "I hope I don't see or hear anything!" As a result, my sleep was a bit troubled. My wife, on the other hand, had no problem sleeping at all.

I saw/heard nothing except what you would expect in a 199-year-old building. I hope to sleep a little better tonight. Will likely leave a light on! *(P.S. The guy playing "Dixie" on the banjo all last night didn't help, either...)*

*J*uly 31, 1996 {Day 2}: Last night, we kept a light on all night and the air conditioner running. We both slept better. No sightings or sounds to report. It was a very interesting stay for us. We enjoyed ourselves very much!

*O*ctober 4, 1996: My husband and I are visiting from Massachusetts. We came to visit Gettysburg, but didn't realize what a big part the Cashtown Inn would play! We didn't know too much about the inn before we came here, and we were pleasantly surprised at its beauty and charm. This room is incredible! The writings on the wall and the decor are really wonderful—you can *feel* the people who have been here over the past 200 years. If we ever come back to this area (which we plan to), we will be staying here.

However, I hope to get more sleep next time! I guess we were a little spooked on finding out that this was the room where most "things" happen.

Chp. B. Brunt hault
august 7. 1835

[Note: The writings on the wall in this room date from the mid-1830s. Evidently, graffiti is not a 20th-century phenomenon. Did A.P. Hill once read these writings?]

We both had trouble sleeping. I heard sounds from near the window (where the rocking chair is). The next morning, I found out that my husband heard noises as well, but didn't want to scare me. Probably just normal sounds from an old house (plus imagination and nerves). But I *did* get scared awake at 4:50 a.m. by the sound of something dropping on the nightstand next to me (near the fireplace). It woke me up from a dead sleep as it banged, then faltered. Nothing was there. Needless to say, we were up for the day... Thanks for an unforgettable stay!

October 10, 1996 {Day 1}: This room is very cozy and well-detailed. We really liked the exposed writing on the walls. We feel connected with the antiquity of the building and the area.

No unexplained events to report, except my wife's sleep was very disrupted...perhaps due to a rich late-evening dinner in town??

October 11, 1996 {Day 2}: Spent a wonderful day just sightseeing and visiting the battlefield. Enjoyed dinner at the inn and took an early retirement to our room.

Everything was rather uneventful until exactly 1:56 a.m., when we both heard a door slam hard and then heavy footsteps in the hallway. The steps stopped after a few seconds. We're puzzled as to where they went.

Heard various sounds during the remainder of the night/morning; however, we attribute them to this old building settling.

October 31, 1996 {6:30 a.m.}: I'm so excited! I've been waiting for this Halloween for some time now. I'm convinced that today will be the day for my experience!

We started in the tavern room. Lots of stories from previous visitors. Nothing happening for me yet.

After about an hour and half of being in different spots in the house, we decided to take a short break and have breakfast. We sat at the table near the mirror.

Without any reason, I was suddenly overwhelmed with a rush of intense emotion. I began to cry and did not know why. I got up from the table and walked out the door down the hall, to Rooms 6 and 7. As soon as I passed through the doorway, the feeling left me. It was just as though someone had turned off a switch. I was then able to return to my table.

About ten minutes later, I felt another shudder of emotion, and again, started crying. I got up and left the room through the same doorway, again, "turning off the switch." At this point, my husband was concerned that something was wrong, but I had no explanation for the feelings of overwhelming sadness. I again returned to the table.

It happened once more, a little later during our meal. On—then off. Just totally amazing!

Later in the day, I had the opportunity to talk to a local psychic who was also visiting the inn. She told me that she knew me in a previous life. She said that I was named Georgia and was probably a nurse caring for wounded soldiers. She said she saw me in a basement comforting and tending to the soldiers. This is not so hard for me to believe. When we took a bus tour of the battlefield in July, I visualized a hospital, in a basement, with immense pain and suffering. I cried on the bus then, too.

Gettysburg keeps drawing us back. We will return again and, someday, I will be writing in another journal—hopefully, with more of an understanding of the sadness I feel here.

November 1, 1996 {Day 1}: My wife and I were enjoying our stay here and were blissfully ignorant of the ghost stories surrounding the inn. Following a day of hiking around Gettysburg, we returned to the inn for a quick nap before dinner. I heard a noise near the rocking chair and attributed it to something falling or shifting. Neither my wife nor I fell asleep during our nap; we just rested quietly with the radio on.

My wife got up and began to move around quietly, thinking I was asleep, since she said she heard me "snoring." I had *not* fallen asleep and did not hear the snoring.

November 2, 1996 {Day 2}: Last night, at exactly 2:36 a.m., I felt someone get up off the edge of the bed (as if someone were sitting at my side—it was very strange). I had not read this journal before hearing the noise in the corner or the "snoring" incident, so when I read the accounts in this book and learned the history of this room, it was a bit haunting.

This is a wonderful inn, with kind, gracious hosts. We *will* return!

November 22-24, 1996: This was a big weekend! Not only was it my girlfriend's birthday weekend, but I planned on asking her to marry me, as well! All went well in that department—we are now engaged!!

No unusual events on Friday night. I was up most of the night listening and watching from bed. All I heard was random "old house" noises, with the exception of a series of three taps coming from somewhere in the front of the room, at about 1:30 a.m.

Saturday night was an active and strange night. On the front porch swing, I asked my girlfriend to marry me. When we came in, we were greeted by Eileen, who was the first one to hear the happy news. She told us that the inn was filled with loves and ghost hunters—my fiancée and I, a newlywed couple, and three groups of ghost hunters. We took a small bottle of champagne to our room (compliments of the Hoovers) and toasted our life together.

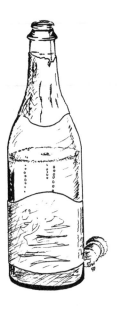

The night certainly was not a quiet one. The ghost hunters were very active in the hallway. The ghost in Room 3 also became active! Maybe it was the full moon! Sometime shortly after midnight, I awoke to a banging noise. I then sat and listened for the next 20 minutes as an unseen "ghost" frolicked in the front left corner of the room.

Earlier in the evening, I placed the ice bucket, bottles, and glasses on the table. I could now clearly hear the water and ice in the bucket sloshing around. This did not occur just once, but frequently. I also heard other rustling noises from the corner. At one point, I even thought I heard our "guest" walk across the room, but I suppose it could have been echoes from the hallway.

After these noises stopped, I began to hear noises in the bathroom. I guess the noises could have been coming from the room on the other side of the bathroom, but they certainly sounded like they were coming from the bathroom. The rest of the night was quiet.

Anyway, so much for my ghost experience! We had an absolutely wonderful weekend. I guarantee that we will be back many times!!!

J **anuary 4, 1997 {Day 1}:** This inn is great! I can't say enough good things about it or the Hoovers!

However...strange noises all night long! Banging and a "shriek" about 1 a.m. One hour prior, at midnight, the alarm clock went off all by itself. When I turned on the light to investigate, it flickered and went out. The bathroom door opened by itself. Also, at 3 a.m., we heard footsteps on the staircase and landing outside the room. We also heard conversation noises and footsteps on the floor above—it sounded like someone moving furniture. Noises persisted until 5 a.m.

At dawn, I could have sworn I heard horses in the street below (any Amish families in the area?)

January 5, 1997 {Day 2}: My husband and I enjoyed this inn and our hosts. We really felt like we were visiting family!

Staying in this room with all the sounds was an experience all its own! The clock, light, voices, odd sounds, tapping—one noise sounded almost like someone crying out in pain. I felt a very cold draft around me, while my husband, in the meantime, was sweating bullets (mostly from me clinging onto him for dear life).

Also, at 11:30 p.m. last night, we locked the room door and chained it; this morning, the chain was off and the door was unlocked!

We will be back again, but I think we'll choose another room!

February 9, 1997: We had a lovely visit here at the Cashtown Inn. We were very comfortable in our room; no ghosts, but we did hear some unusual noises—a moaning from the room behind ours (no one was in that room) and a tapping or drumming sound from the porch.

We'll definitely be back again. Thanks for the gracious hospitality!

F ebruary 22 1997: Don't read this book [the guest journal in each room] before you go to bed! *(P.S. Don't let the person you're with read this book before you go to bed, either, because you won't get any sleep!)*

M arch 6, 1997 {Day 1}: Arrived today at 3 p.m. sharp. After my wife and I finished unpacking, she went into the bathroom to freshen up. I went out to the hall to look at the print of Joshua Chamberlain. Suddenly, from behind the closed bathroom door, I heard my wife yell, "That wasn't funny! You scared me to death!" I came back into the room just as she was coming out of the bathroom. She burst into a barrage of accusations. I found myself being tried and sentenced for pounding on the bathroom door!

(It is now 9:20 p.m. and I'm not sure she believes that I was not the one who pounded on the door. Let me assure you, dear reader, that I was *not* in the room at the time, and that I heard nothing!)

Shortly after the first incident, my wife heard a tapping sound coming from the wall, near the rocking chair; but alas, I was outside taking pictures of the inn.

We are turning in for the night now. I guess I'll know in the morning if I offend the spirits enough to keep them away...

M arch 7, 1997 {Day 2}: When we awoke this morning, the bathroom door was still closed, the chain was still on the door, and a glass of water was still on the nightstand, untouched.

The tapping I heard yesterday was the furnace; the banging in the bathroom I cannot explain. Nor can I explain my restless night and the feeling that we were not alone. I can't help but think that if I had left my husband at home, maybe I would have encountered something supernatural. *(P.S. The question still remains: Did my husband bang on the bathroom door or not??)*

> *Shortly after moving into the inn, both innkeepers were awakened at 1 a.m. by the sound of a loud crash outside their bedroom window. Thinking it was a car crash, they looked out the window up and down the street. Nothing was amiss on the highway, but they noticed that all the books on the top shelf of their bedroom bookcase had been thrown onto the floor!?!*

March 23, 1997: I'm pressed for time this morning, but I wanted to let you know that last night *did* produce some disturbing sounds. I did not read any journal entries prior to this morning; but everything in the entry dated May 15, 1996, happened to my husband and me, as well. I am normally a very skeptical person, but it really *did* happen!

ROOM 4
MAJ. GEN. HARRY HETH

May 11, 1996: As my husband and I turned off the bedside lamp, "something invisible" whizzed through the air!!

After whistling "Dixie," we spent a comfortable night with no further strange occurrences.

Suggest you state your allegiance upon entering this room!

Sleep well and sweet dreams!

May 20, 1996 {Day 1}: I was very tired upon arriving back to our room. I fell asleep almost immediately. While I was sleeping, it felt like somebody was nudging me. I was sleeping on the left side of the bed, near the door, next to Maj. Gen. George Pickett's portrait. My husband was lying on the right side of the bed. What was odd was that the nudging seemed to be coming from underneath me and to my right (by the wall with Pickett's picture) and I was being pushed toward my husband. It was *not* coming from the side of the bed that my husband was on. It then stopped for a while. Suddenly, I felt as though somebody picked me up from underneath and threw me. I landed on the bed toward the center! My husband then said something, but I was so exhausted, I don't remember what he said, and I fell right back to sleep.

(I was sleeping on the bed next to my wife, but she kept bumping into me and eventually woke me up. I was listening to my Walkman, when suddenly the bed depressed next to me (underneath my wife) and she sprang up and flipped, then landed on the bed. The whole time her body stayed perfectly parallel to the bed, as if she were lying on a straight board with her hands at her side. She rose at least three to four inches off the bed—she was actually in the air! She then spun and crashed back onto the bed. It looked as though somebody had spring-loaded her, like a catapult. It reminded me of the old movies when the sheets are pulled out from underneath somebody, except she was in the air at the time. By the way, this all occurred between 5 and 6 a.m.)

May 21, 1996 {Day 2}: It was a little after 6 this morning when I got up to take a shower. I was in the shower stall when I asked my husband to turn the light out and close the door. When the door was open I would get a breeze in the shower, and the lights were blinding me (I was still waking up). He did as I asked and went back into the bedroom.

It was very dark in the bathroom and as I was shampooing my hair, I felt a cold breeze on my back. I looked up over the shower rod and noticed that there was light in the bathroom (as if the door was open and the light from the bedroom was pouring in). I assumed that my husband had walked in to get something, so I just continued my shower.

When I came out, I was a bit annoyed and asked him if he was trying to get me sick. He gave me a bewildered look and asked me what I was talking about. When I told him, he said he never went into the bathroom and the door was never opened. When I reflected on what happened, I realized that I never heard the door open and it was clicked all the way closed when I went to exit the bathroom. I guess I just assumed the door had opened because of the cold breeze.

Later, I also realized that when you walk into the bathroom, the floor creaks. I did *not* hear the floor creak during that "encounter."

May 31, 1996 {Day 1}: As soon as we approached the Cashtown Inn, I knew that we would have a wonderful time. The inn exudes a wonderful personality. There is much "activity" here. There are a lot of comings and goings on the porch— mainly men in Civil War uniforms who have left their signature energy behind. As we walked up the stairs, I saw a white gaseous (female) energy. She seemed to be in her late 20s to early 30s.

The Hoovers are wonderful hosts. Dennis showed us the rooms before the rest of the guests arrived. Various psychics have been through the inn. I do not consider myself a psychic, but I am very sensitive and can "see" a lot of things.

There is a tall man up in the rafters, in the suite upstairs. He stands with shoulders stooped, dressed in a ragged cloak. It is the turn of the 19th century—winter. I see snow outside and it is cold—a feeling of desperation—and the man does not know where to turn. It is a matter of survival. There is hay strewn in the room and that is where the family sleeps. The assumption is that he is related to the "dirty, poorly clad woman and child" who are seen in one of the rooms. The entire scene is sad and ended as such.

At 1:30 a.m., I was awakened by a draft of air across my right cheek, and my ear "popped." I have had trouble with my right ear for some time and it bothers me when the weather changes. This was not the case this time, and my ear has never popped in this manner. I felt the mattress at the bottom of the bed move up (no sound was made), as if someone was pushing it up with their fist. I

also felt someone nudging me with a hand on my back, as if they wanted me to move over because there was no room for them. It was definitely not my husband, because he was sound asleep, facing the opposite wall.

June 1, 1996 {Day 2}: The same thing happened as the previous night. About 2:30 a.m., I awoke feeling a hand pushing up from the bottom of the mattress at the foot of the bed. I also felt the gentle nudging of someone's hand on my back, as if they wanted me to move over.

There are two male energies in the basement. I was not able to get a fix on them as they ran to another part of the basement and disappeared into the wall.

June 2-5, 1996: My husband is an avid history buff— primarily with the Civil War—and coming to Gettysburg was his lifelong dream. I just wanted to see a ghost! Well, if life isn't ironic enough, I became suddenly interested in all of the details of the Civil War during our stay, and my husband—the skeptic—saw a ghost! It was approximately 1:30 a.m. on Monday, when we were both startled from our sleep by a loud thud from the center of our room (and it was not the air conditioner)! I actually tried to stay awake after that, but could not. Apparently, my husband could, because just seconds after I closed my eyes, he sat straight up and said, "Did you see that?" Doesn't it figure??!!

Our shade above the air conditioner was raised slightly, so the light from the parking lot created a shadow of the window on the wall by the door. After I began to doze, my husband glanced at the lighted "window" on the wall and saw the distinct figure of a Confederate soldier (because of the type of hat worn) walk across the shadow. Needless to say, he was terrified the rest of the night! The following night, I had several strange "dreams," to say the least.

Thanks to the Hoovers, who are wonderful hosts. We enjoyed our stay and will be back!

June 21, 1996: By 10:30 p.m., we had read all the magazines, talked about the day's events, and planned the next day's schedule. I turned out the light with the hope of getting a good night's sleep, trying to dismiss from my mind all previous entries in this journal that described strange occurrences between 1 and 5 a.m.

As luck would have it, we fell asleep immediately. Like I said, as luck would have it... My wife and I were both startled by the air conditioner re-energizing itself at approximately 1 a.m. I was awake for most of the night between 1 and 4 a.m., with my mind and eyes both wandering. It's funny how every shadow dances just enough to speed your heart rate; and the drone of the air conditioner can, at times, sound like someone walking above you. My wife later told me that she, too, didn't sleep much, as she was also remembering previous journal entries.

We were here to celebrate our first anniversary together, as well as our love for each other. We fully anticipate coming back next year. Hopefully, having already spent a night here will provide for better rest at that time!

No ghost sightings to report, but you never know what happens the second you close your eyes!

July 7, 1996: After reading about the ghosts of the Cashtown Inn, I was expecting a very long night. It was, but only because the air conditioner did not work and it was 100 degrees! As far as I'm concerned, there are no such things as ghosts—just people with wild imaginations, like my wife.

(Unlike my husband, I do believe in ghosts! At about 4:30 a.m., I saw a man in a gray uniform leaning over the desk, looking for something. He was very tall, with blondish-white hair, and he was smiling. By then, I was so tired that all I could do was turn over and try to go back to sleep!)

July 14, 1996: My wife and I came to the Cashtown Inn anticipating nothing and expecting anything. After reading the previous narratives, we came to the conclusion that *anything* could happen. Did we see or hear strange things? To be honest—not really. However, this inn has its own spirit, and you can sense that this establishment has a place in history. If the walls could only talk!

If you lay still in bed, the quiet will engulf you, and you will understand that you are a part of this inn's history. The creaking of the floors, the quiet moan of the air conditioner during the summer—all will add to the experience.

For the next guests who stay in Room 4—good luck in seeing a ghost, if that is what you are here for. More importantly, enjoy the history and hospitality this inn offers!

July 31, 1996: We are here to visit Gettysburg. When we first walked into this room, we heard somebody

breathing heavily over our shoulders...it happened twice.
Later that night, when we were asleep—about 2:30 a.m.—
I heard a loud bang!

> *The innkeeper was showing a group of*
> *three ladies around the guest rooms. Dis-*
> *appointed that Room #4 was rented for the*
> *night, one guest remarked that she wanted*
> *to see a ghost. The innkeeper replied that*
> *spirits seem to roam the entire inn and*
> *could be anywhere. The guest said, "Just*
> *think, there could be a ghost here right*
> *now." At that moment, her earring shot*
> *out of her earlobe projectile-style and*
> *dropped onto the floor several feet from*
> *her.*

November 24, 1996: What a wonderfully warm atmosphere and great hospitality! We were on edge all
evening, knowing the stories that surround this place.
Coming from educationally sound backgrounds and being
active Catholics, we still kept an open mind, just in case we
might experience something. There was no doubt—we
were afraid!

A violently swinging porch swing with no strong wind
or person in sight set us up for an evening of fright! De-
spite a night-light left on in our room, we sensed a presence, and both my husband and I heard the lamp (or something) thud multiple times. The windows, left open a few
inches throughout the night, let in distant marching
sounds that we heard twice. Although we have strong be-
liefs in God and the hereafter, we feel that "spirits" or
something can exist for some unknown reason.

Our advice: Keep an open mind and enjoy your stay.
We sure did! We will be back!

December 8, 1996: Well, it's Sunday morning and we're still here!

This is our first visit to the Cashtown Inn. I'm a person who tends to see more than what is apparent, and my husband is a huge Civil War buff.

We were both very aware of the ghostly sightings reported and, needless to say, I was terrified at the thought of sleeping in Room 4. I fortified myself with a few drinks and we went up to bed. It seemed like hours before either of us was able to sleep. I dozed off about 2 a.m.; my husband stayed awake until almost 3 a.m.

Prior to going to bed, I needed to use the bathroom. I pulled the shade cord down and it broke. I put it down on the window sill and when I looked for it again, it was gone. I found it under the shade on the window top.

After going to bed, it was fairly uneventful until about 5 a.m., when we both heard footsteps on the stairs, the sound of something dragging from one end to the other from the room above, and someone talking. At one point, the footsteps seemed to approach our room, as if to enter, but stopped right at the door.

So, after what seemed like an eternity of banging, dragging, and talking, at about 6:30 a.m., we finally dozed off again.

All in all, I was not as terrified as I thought I would be, but I think we'll choose another room next time!

December 22, 1996: This was our first time at the Cashtown Inn. We've heard all the stories and unbelievable tales about the inn, and we were both anxious to see or hear something that would be in accordance with the tales.

At 2:07 a.m., we awoke to a loud rapping on the window. After we sat there in bed for a few minutes, it happened again...and again. This went on until about 5 a.m. All through the night, we both heard footsteps, but could not tell where they were coming from.

February 7, 1997: This is our first time at the Cashtown Inn. We heard noises coming from the left side of the bed, as well as from behind the chair and dresser.

I felt a depression at the foot of the bed (on the left side). This happened not once, but several times. The clincher was when I came off the bed, straight up, about three inches! This was *not* the same as being startled in my sleep!

I'm glad it's now morning. I'm still shaking and I'm going home now. But I hope to be back, now that I know what to expect. Sleep tight!

February 20, 1997: This was our first visit to the Cashtown Inn. We heard a lot about the inn and Room 4 from several television shows.

During the night, my husband and I thought we heard breathing coming from above the door entrance. We also heard tapping on the ceiling around 2:30 a.m. However, once we finally fell asleep, we slept fine. I videotaped during the night and took some pictures. When I play back the recording and develop the pictures, maybe I'll have something paranormal to show. I hope to come back here again to do more investigating!

We really enjoyed our visit and will definitely return again soon!

> *The exhausted innkeepers climbed into bed one night, prepared to turn off their bedside lamps. Suddenly, their closed and latched bathroom door began to vibrate violently, as though someone was trying to shake it off its hinges. This phenomenon continued for about a minute.*

April 5, 1997 {Day 1}: My sisters and I have all heard the stories about Room 4. We are fascinated by the occult/supernatural, so we practically prayed that something strange would happen. We waited patiently, and about midnight, things started to happen.

First, the room was unbelievably hot. We looked for an air conditioner. We knew one was in the room, because we had heard stories about it. While I searched, one of my sisters went into the bathroom. She closed the door behind her, but she did not lock it. Suddenly, I heard her rattle the door and yell, "Help me, I'm locked in!" She fiddled with the door for about two minutes before she was finally released.

Meanwhile, we continued to search for the air conditioner; we gave up after a while. I was sitting in the chair, one of my sisters was lying on the bed, and my other sister was on the floor. Suddenly, the small night-light on the window sill fell to the ground. No one was near the cord or the light at the time.

We will keep you posted on further events, as I brought along cards that we can use to "talk" to the spirits. We plan to do this between 1 and 5 a.m., because that seems to be when the spirits are most active.

April 6, 1997 {Day 2}: We used the cards last night. A ghost seemed willing to talk to us!

After putting my cards away, strange noises plagued us all through the night.

We really enjoyed our stay in Room 4. We'll be back!

(P.S. One last thing...The shower curtain blew in on my sister when she took her shower, and it did the same with me.)

ROOM 5
GEN. ROBERT E. LEE

May 12-13, 1996: My wife and I came here as hon-
eymooners, having been married the previous day.
We had a wonderful stay!

As far as any "bumps in the night," we heard some
creaks and cracks, and cold breezes coming from the windows. Also, whether it was simply our imaginations or not,
while sitting on the couch at about 10 p.m., we both heard
a distinct breathing sound coming from the corner by the
window. We looked at each other in amazement, and when
I stood up and headed in that direction, it quickly stopped.
That is all in terms of anything that remotely resembled a
supernatural experience.

We hope to return someday and truly encounter a
ghostly being. We hope everyone who follows us has a
pleasant and memorable stay!

May 27, 1996: This is our third visit to the Cashtown
Inn in the last three months. Our first visit was back
in March.

On the second evening of our stay, I remembered that
Eileen and Dennis had left us two bottles of Perrier water in
the refrigerator and, being thirsty, I decided to open one of
the bottles. I then realized that the bottle did not have a
twist-off cap and that I would need a bottle opener. However,
there was no bottle opener in the room. I went downstairs

to look for one, but since it was almost midnight, nobody was around to help me. Still determined to drink my Perrier, I went back up to the room and tried to pry off the cap with my keys...no success. I finally gave up, put the bottle down on the table, and then took a glass from the bathroom and filled it with tap water. The next morning, as I was packing my bag, my wife said to me, "I see you got the Perrier open." I told her I didn't and went over to the table where I had left the bottle. The cap was still on tight, but the water was almost completely gone! We couldn't believe it. My first attempt at a logical explanation was evaporation, but that much water cannot evaporate in six or seven hours. The water in the glass hadn't even evaporated. Our only other explanation was a thirsty ghost with a sense of humor, showing me how easily he or she could drink the water.

All of my stays at the inn have been very pleasant and I will return again!

(P.S. Now there's a bottle opener in the room!)

48

May 30, 1996 {Mother}: I enjoyed a very memorable stay in Room 5 with my two daughters. Just being present where history took place so many years ago was "encounter" enough for me, although there was the unexplained "scratching" (or some facsimile thereof) in the corner by the window in the sitting room of the suite.

To other guests who follow, I truly hope you enjoy your stay!

May 30, 1996 {Daughter 1}: Being open-minded, yet somewhat skeptical, I felt apprehensive about staying here overnight in the original structure of the inn, and most especially, being the only guests in the entire inn. I was afraid we would be "magnets" for the spirits in the suite on the top floor! I was waiting for "Grandma" to brush by the bed in the night, but I was afraid to look. My sister wanted to venture down to Rooms 1 to 4 because it was an empty floor, but fear took over. She felt she missed the chance of a lifetime for an encounter. In reality, I experienced nothing supernatural—I was disappointed, yet relieved of my fears.

I would definitely choose the Cashtown Inn as a place to stay again because of its history, apparitions, and suspense, not to mention the fact that it is a very nice inn! Thank you, Dennis, Eileen, and staff!

May 30, 1996 {Daughter 2}: I am in my glory! This was such an enjoyable stay! My mom, my sister, and I were the only visitors staying here last night. I was elected to sleep by myself on the fold-out couch. The room most definitely seemed different at night than during the day.

I left the TV on, with the movie *Gettysburg* playing, just for sound, and I had a small flashlight to read by. My pillows propped, I suddenly felt a gentle poke through the back of my pillow, which touched the side of my head. I brushed the thought away, being unsure of what I had just felt. As I continued to read, it happened again. It was a very gentle touch, but my heart was pounding! I left the TV running and—*yes*—climbed in with Mom and Sis! We laughed, thinking about the three of us in one bed, like the Three Stooges!

On the day we arrived, we were given a tour of the inn, including the rooms. Room 3 had a very strong smell of a pleasant powder (no doubt about it). This morning, on my way down for breakfast, I visited all four rooms again; this time, there was no scent in Room 3. Later in the day, before we checked out, we again entered Room 3...the pleasant scent was back!

I enjoyed my stay immensely! I will be back! (But not alone!)

> *It is believed that during the Civil War, nicotine-craving Confederate soldiers picked unripe tobacco leaves from nearby farmers' fields and rolled their own "green" cigars. The innkeeper thinks she knows what they must have smelled like, because four times in 1997 she had "phantom" cigar smoke blown into her face. Each time, the inn was closed and she was alone. And each time, she called to her husband to come verify the smell, but he was not able to smell it.*

June 24-26, 1996: I was here two years ago with my 15-year-old son and had such a great time that I knew I'd be back (we live in the San Francisco Bay area).

My wife is with me this time. She was completely surprised. (I guess she thought any place my son and I stayed would be a little primitive.)

We had a wonderful time seeing all the sights and relaxing each evening. Unfortunately, no ghost sightings.

However, when I was here before, my son slept on the left side of the bed and I was on the right. I woke up in the middle of the night facing my son. All of a sudden, he bolted straight up in bed and looked wildly into the other room. "Who are you? What do you want?" he said very firmly, staring straight into the sitting room. I frankly was too nervous—all right *afraid*—to look! He asked again, "What do you want?" and then laid back down.

I don't know if it was a ghost or a dream, but I did feel uncomfortable enough not to look to check it out!

Thanks for the wonderful time. We'll be back!

July 2, 1996: This is a wonderful place...very beautiful! We did not see or hear any ghosts, but we did have *dreams* about ghosts. Does that count??

August 3, 1996: Although we saw nothing out of the ordinary (with my family being slightly more relieved than disappointed over this), I had a strong sense that there was something or someone here with us—a presence; nothing, though, to be fearful of.

The Cashtown Inn is a wonderful place full of history, but it was the warm hospitality of the Hoovers that we enjoyed most. We will return some day. Best of luck!

October 27, 1996: What a wonderful way to spend a first anniversary! A Halloween wedding with its first celebration at a "haunted" inn...we loved it!

The "night life" is active around here. We both heard several doors open and close downstairs in the early a.m. hours (3 to 4), and as far as we knew, we were the only guests! *Someone* also seems to be very security-conscious. The chain lock on our door was rattled around 4 a.m.

The Cashtown Inn is fantastic. We can't wait to come back!

(P.S. We also think our wine glasses were of interest to someone. We remember hearing glass tapping, and it was too high a pitch for the windows!)

November 22-23, 1996: What a fantastic weekend! My two grown daughters, an uncle, an aunt, and I shared Room 5.

We videotaped a lot of fantastic sights! We all heard and experienced these sights and sounds together. If you are not a believer now, stay in Room 5 and you will become a believer, for sure!

We heard heavy breathing and smelled something *stale* in the air. It came from the window by the television. I felt someone touch my head, and the side of my face was rubbed gently.

During the evening, one of my daughters and I went downstairs to the parlor, where we were joined by a man who was staying in Room 2. As we talked, all the hall lights went out. All three of us heard something or someone running up and down the stairs, and there was a very loud banging of doors. We all looked up the stairs and tried to turn the lights back on, but *nothing!* Everything was still.

Earlier that evening, after dinner, several patrons were in the parlor, talking. The swing on the front porch started to swing frantically all by itself. No one was on it and there was no wind to speak of. It swung so high, it was making a jerking motion. Several of us headed outside to get a closer look, but as soon as we stepped out the door, it stopped dead!

We had a wonderful time and we enjoyed the warmth and hospitality extended by the Hoovers. We will definitely return!

January 13, 1997 {Day 1}: So here I am, on my birthday! I've always wanted to stay here. This is my birthday present from my husband who, at the present moment, is snoozing contentedly on the sofa. I have the *Gettysburg* movie playing as I write; it just seemed appropriate! We are the only guests here tonight, so we have the place to ourselves...maybe??!!

The whole place just seems to have a vibe about it, but it's not an uncomfortable feeling. I have to admit, I was a little apprehensive at first—so many stories!

We live near Chambersburg, in a house that is said to have been where the Confederates met before they burned Chambersburg. And of course, we have our own resident ghost, whom we call "Sara." My husband has seen her; the cats have seen her. Unfortunately, *I* haven't seen her. But the vibe here is the same vibe I feel at our house...that feeling of not being alone.

What a great place! Oh, and if you've read through this journal...the swing story is true! I was here with a friend about two years ago. The place was closed, so we were peeking in the windows to see what we could see. With absolutely *no* wind that day, the swing just started to swing steadily. As we made tracks to the car, it came to a dead stop! (Please excuse the pun.)

I guess it's time for bed. I wonder what kind of dreams I'll have tonight?

January 14, 1997 {Day 2}: Well, nothing eventful happened during the night. However, I *did* stay up until 2 a.m., watching the *Gettysburg* movie! So once I did finally fall asleep, I guess I could have slept through anything!

We are heading out to the battlefield, then home. I can't wait to return!

In compiling this book, we needed to get some photos of the different rooms in the Cashtown Inn as an aid for the artist to render sketches. My family was in town and they agreed to help. As we drove to the inn, we talked about the haunts there and about how the prospect of "seeing" something made all of us a little nervous. While secretly hoping that we would experience something, I can say that we were not let down. In the short time we were there, two doors opened by themselves. And when a camera I had placed on a table in the upstairs hallway went off by itself, we all became true believers. Did the spirits want to help with the photos?

—Bob Wasel

April 6, 1997: Unfortunately, I experienced no strange occurrences. However, I did have an absolutely wonderful weekend here! The "homey" atmosphere of this room made me feel extremely comfortable. Everyone here was especially nice, also. I look forward to returning sometime soon.

(My wife may not have experienced anything strange; however, I did! We went to bed around 1 a.m. My wife turned the heat up right before we fell asleep. Around 4 a.m., I woke up and found the room to be very, very warm. I thought to myself, "I wish it wasn't so hot!"

Just then, as I was lying on the left side of the bed, I felt a breath of strong and deliberate cool air come over my face and hands. It did not feel like steady air conditioning or a draft from a window, as my wife would have me believe. It was more like the gentle breath of someone who has cooled many brows over the years.)

May 5, 1997: As my sister and I prepare to leave the inn (our third visit), we, of course, pass on our best wishes to the Hoovers. Each time we stay here, we love it more and more! Aside from the pleasant atmosphere, just to spend time in a place that holds so much history is thought-provoking and awesome in itself, making it a treasurable memory.

We did not experience any strange activity, yet it may have existed around us and we did not notice it. (A woman's faint, muffled cry in the far-off distance while I was sitting on the love seat by the window had me wondering, though!)

This room is charming. If there are spirits roaming here at the Cashtown Inn, they have provided nothing but happy and friendly emotions.

God bless this home and inn. I feel comfort and goodness in this place!

POSTSCRIPT

While we were putting this book together, the Hoovers received an interesting letter from some former guests, regarding a photo they had taken at the inn. The letter read:

Dear Dennis / Eileen:

I doubt that you remember my family (myself and my daughter Shanna and son Colin); we stayed at your Cashtown Inn this August. We certainly enjoyed the evening and your hosting a tour of the inn the next morning. We stayed in the Robert E. Lee Room and were especially taken by the history of the house and that room.

I am writing to express an unusual request. Could you examine the attached photographic enlargement of a portion of your sitting room (you may keep it for your collection of "hard-to-explain" occurrences associated with the Cashtown Inn) and tell me if the figure superimposed on the photograph appears anywhere else in that room...or in the inn for that matter.

The photo was taken during the daytime and does not show any other image but the soldier dressed in a long coat and standing on or in front of the rock in the picture. He appears to be a "holographic" image, without any accompanying background that would indicate some sort of double exposure of the film.

The film we used was a very high-speed type, which we had not used before, and evidently picked up something that we didn't see at the time of the picture. I am particularly interested in the narrative you recounted of the rebel soldier appearing in the photo taken of the front of the inn at an earlier time in its history. Did that soldier look anything like the one in [our] photo?

In any case, the attached photo is a curiosity, which has only made our visit to your inn that much more memorable. We hope to hear from you soon.

Very truly yours,

Colin and William Clister
Canton, GA

Did the Clisters capture a ghost on film? Or is the "soldier in the glass" merely a photographic glitch? What do *you* think??

Have you experienced strange, supernatural, or unexplainable occurrences in Gettysburg? If so, we would like to hear about it for possible inclusion in future publications about Haunted Gettysburg. Please include only firsthand experiences and, if available, photographs you have taken personally. This is your chance to tell your story without fear of ridicule. You are not alone—hundreds, perhaps thousands, of people have had some sort of unexplained "ghostly" experience in Gettysburg. If you would like your story told, please fill out and sign the release form and send it to the address indicated for potential inclusion. If your story is used, you will receive a free, personally autographed copy of the book. Your name will be used unless you specifically request otherwise.

Material/Photo Release

To: Gettysburg R&D

P.O. Box 4561

Gettysburg, PA 17325

I hereby grant to Suzanne Gruber and Bob Wasel the absolute right and permission to reproduce the material and/or photographs I have supplied to them for inclusion in Haunted Gettysburg and in future reprints and revisions. I further consent to the publication and copyrighting of this book to be published in any manner they may see fit. Proper acknowledgment of my material and/or photos will be made at the authors' discretion.

Name _____

Address _____

_____

_____

Date _____

Signature _____